100 facts Science

D0520922

100 facts Science

Steve Parker

Consultant: Peter Riley

Miles Kelly

First published in 2005 by Miles Kelly Publishing Ltd
Harding's Barn, Bardfield End Green, Thaxted, Essex, CM6 3PX, UK

Copyright © Miles Kelly Publishing 2005

This edition printed in 2012

2 4 6 8 10 9 7 5 3

Publishing Director Belinda Gallagher
Creative Director Jo Cowan
Editorial Director Rosie McGuire
Editorial Assistant Lauren White
Designer Kayleigh Allen
Production Manager Elizabeth Collins
Reprographics Stephan Davis, Thom Allaway
Assets Lorraine King

All rights reserved. No part of this publication may be reproduced,
stored in a retrieval system, or transmitted by any means, electronic,
mechanical, photocopying, recording or otherwise, without the
prior permission of the copyright holder.

ISBN 978-1-84810-627-7

Printed in China

British Library Cataloguing-in-Publication Data
A catalogue record for this book is available from the British Library

ACKNOWLEDGEMENTS

The publishers would like to thank the following sources for the use of their photographs:
Key: t = top, b = bottom, c = centre, l = left, r = right, m = main, bg = background

Cover (front) James Doss/Shutterstock, (back) Silverstore/Dreamstime, higyou/Shutterstock
Dreamstime 18 Silverstore; 19(bg) Adam1975, 21(t) Paha_l; 34(tr) Zoom-zoom
Fotolia 13(tl) Paul Heasman, (cr) Dariusz Kopestynski; 21(b) photlook; 34(third from tr)
iStock 16–17(bg) Kevin Smith   **Photolibrary** 19(b) Laguna Design
Shutterstock 6–7 ssguy; 8–9 Sergey Lavrentev; 9(t) Ljupco Smokovski; 10(bg) Deymos, (tr) Vakhrushev Pavel,
(b) Ivonne Wierink; 11(t) w shane dougherty; 12(tr) yuyangc; 14(m) yxm2008, (bl) ARENA Creative;
15(b) Tatiana Makotra; 20(bg) asharkyu, (cr) Eimantas Buzasl; 22–23(m) vadim kozlovsky; 24–25(bg) Gunnar Pippel;
24(b) Smileus; 25(c) Ray Hub; 26(c) Sebastian Crocker; 27(b) Hywit Dimyadi; 28–29(bg) archibald, (c) ifong;
29(tl) Viktor Gmyria; 30–31(bg) Redshinestudio; 31(all) Annette Shaff; 32 Jaggat; 33(c) michael rubin;
34(second from tr) Maksim Toome, (from fourth from tr) Balazs Toth, CaptureLight, Jaochainoi; 40(tl) Kurhan,
(br) Tamara Kulikova; 41(t) Alexander Raths, (b) Kirsty Pargeter; 43(t) wim claes, (b) indiangypsy;
44(m) beerkoff, (bl) Smit; 47(tr) Morgan Lane Photography, (b) ssuaphotos

All other photographs are from:
Corel, digitalSTOCK, digitalvision, John Foxx, PhotoAlto, PhotoDisc,
PhotoEssentials, PhotoPro, Stockbyte

All artworks are from the Miles Kelly Artwork Bank

Every effort has been made to acknowledge the source and copyright holder of each picture.
Miles Kelly Publishing apologises for any unintentional errors or omissions.

Made with paper from a sustainable forest

www.mileskelly.net

info@mileskelly.net

www.factsforprojects.com

Contents

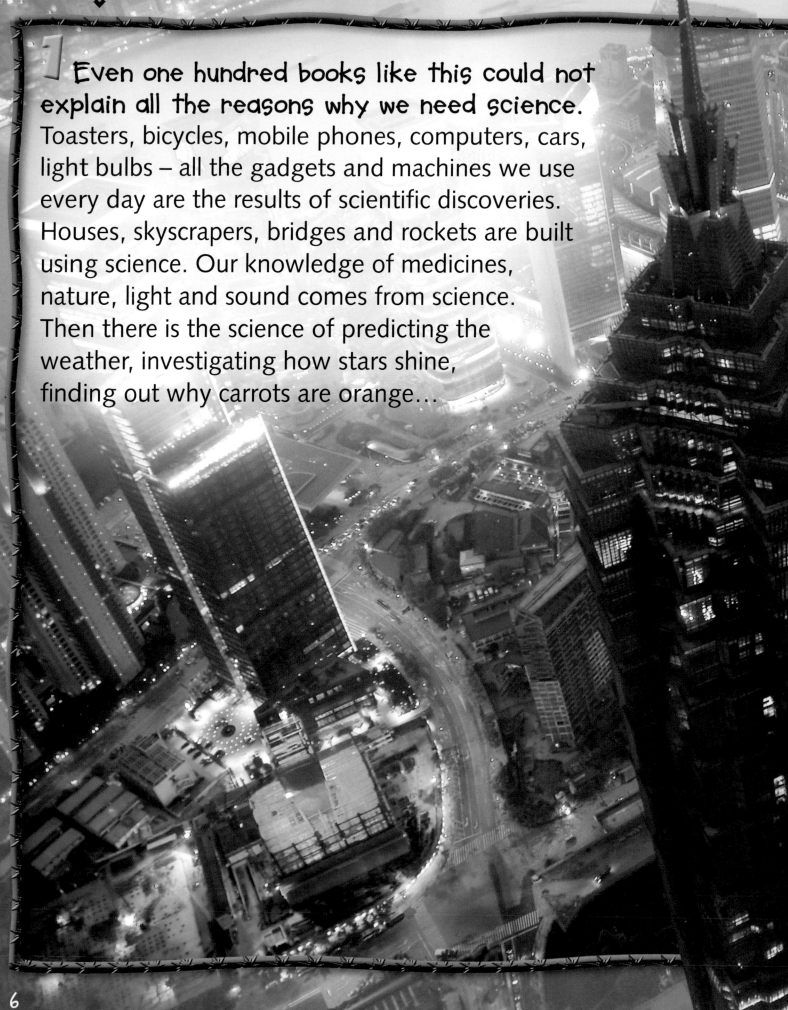

Why do we need science?

1 Even one hundred books like this could not explain all the reasons why we need science. Toasters, bicycles, mobile phones, computers, cars, light bulbs – all the gadgets and machines we use every day are the results of scientific discoveries. Houses, skyscrapers, bridges and rockets are built using science. Our knowledge of medicines, nature, light and sound comes from science. Then there is the science of predicting the weather, investigating how stars shine, finding out why carrots are orange…

▼ In a big city, science is all around you — everything from sky-scraping buildings to speedy vehicles and useful gadgets is based on science and technology.

Machines big and small

2 **Machines are everywhere!** They help us do things, or make doing them easier. Every time you play on a see-saw, you are using a machine! A lever is a stiff bar that tilts at a point called the pivot or fulcrum. The pivot of the see-saw is in the middle. Using the see-saw as a lever, a small person can lift a big person by sitting further from the pivot.

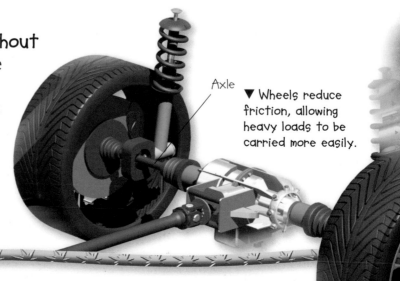

▶ On a see-saw lever, the pivot is in the middle. Other levers have pivots at the end.

Thread

▶ Turning a screw moves it along with more force than the effort used to turn it.

3 **The screw is another simple but useful scientific machine.** It is a ridge, or thread, wrapped around a bar or pole. It changes a small turning motion into a powerful pulling or lifting movement. Wood screws hold together furniture or shelves. A car jack lets you lift up a whole car.

4 **Where would you be without wheels?** Not going very far. The wheel is a simple machine, a circular disc that turns around its centre on a bar called an axle. Wheels carry heavy weights easily. There are giant wheels on big trucks and trains and small wheels on rollerblades.

Axle

▼ Wheels reduce friction, allowing heavy loads to be carried more easily.

▼ Two pulleys together reduce the force needed to lift a heavy girder by one half.

5 **A pulley turns around, like a wheel.** It has a groove around its edge for a cable or rope. Lots of pulleys allow us to lift very heavy weights easily. The pulleys on a tower crane can lift huge steel girders to the top of a skyscraper.

▲ Bicycle gears mean you can pedal at the same speed, with the same force, when climbing up a hill or speeding down it.

Reversing gears

Sliding rack

Pinion gear

Bevel gears

Slow pinion gear

Screw-shaped worm gear

▲ Gears change the turning direction of a force. They can slow it down or speed it up — and even convert it into a sliding force (rack and pinion).

Pivot

Lever

I DON'T BELIEVE IT!

A ramp is a simple machine called an inclined plane. It is easier to walk up a ramp than to jump straight to the top.

6 **Gears are like wheels, with pointed teeth around the edges.** They change a fast, weak turning force into a slow, powerful one – or the other way around. On a bicycle, you can pedal up the steepest hill in bottom (lowest) gear, then speed down the other side in top (highest) gear.

When science is hot!

7 Fire! Flames! Burning! Heat! The science of heat is important in all kinds of ways. Not only do we cook with heat, but we also warm our homes and heat water. Burning happens in all kinds of engines in cars, trucks, planes and rockets. It is also used in factory processes, from making steel to shaping plastics.

▲ A firework burns suddenly as an explosive, producing heat, light and sound. The 'bang' is the sound made by the paper wrapper as it is blown apart.

Heat from the drink is conducted up the metal spoon

8 Heat can move by conduction. A hot object will pass on, or transfer, some of its heat to a cooler one. Dip a metal spoon in a hot drink and the spoon handle soon warms up. Heat is conducted from the drink, through the metal.

9 Heat moves by invisible 'heat rays'. This is called thermal radiation and the rays are infrared waves. Our planet is warmed by the Sun because heat from the Sun radiates through space as infrared waves.

TRUE OR FALSE?

1. Burning happens inside the engine of a plane.
2. A device for measuring temperature is called a calendar.
3. Heat rays are known as infrablue waves.

Answers:
1. True 2. False 3. False

◄ Metal is a good conductor of heat. Put a teaspoon in a hot drink and feel how quickly it heats up.

10 Burning, also called combustion, is a chemical process. Oxygen gas from the air joins to, or combines with, the substance being burned. The chemical change releases lots of heat, and usually light too. If this happens really fast, we call it an explosion.

▲ A burner flame makes glass so hot it becomes soft and bendy, so it can be stretched, shaped and even blown up like a balloon.

11 Temperature is a measure of how hot or cold something is. It is usually measured in degrees Celsius (°C) or Fahrenheit (°F). Water freezes at 0°C (32°F), and boils at 100°C (212°F). We use thermometers to take our temperatures. Your body temperature is about 37°C (98.6°F).

▶ This thermometer contains alcohol coloured by a red dye. As it warms, the alcohol expands (takes up more space). It moves up the thin tube, showing the temperature on the scale.

12 Heat moves through liquids and gases by convection. Some of the liquid or gas takes in heat, gets lighter, and rises into cooler areas. Then other cooler liquid or gas moves in to do the same and the process repeats. You can see this as 'wavy' hot air rising from a flame.

▶ Hot air shimmering over a candle is a visible sign of the heat being convected away.

Engine power

13 Imagine having to walk or run everywhere, instead of riding in a car. Engines are machines that use fuel to do work for us and make life easier. Fuel is a substance that has chemical energy stored inside it. The energy is released as heat by burning or exploding the fuel in the engine.

▼ A jet engine has sets of angled blades, called turbines, that spin on shafts.

Turbines squash incoming air

Jet fuel is sprayed into the air inside the chamber, creating a small explosion

Burning gases spin exhaust turbines

14 Most cars have petrol engines. An air and petrol mixture is pushed into a hollow chamber called a cylinder. A spark from a spark plug makes it explode, which pushes a piston down inside the cylinder. This movement is used by gears to turn the wheels. Most cars have four or six cylinders.

15 A diesel engine doesn't use sparks. The mixture of air and diesel is squashed in the cylinder, becoming so hot it explodes. Diesel engines are used in machines such as tractors that need lots of power.

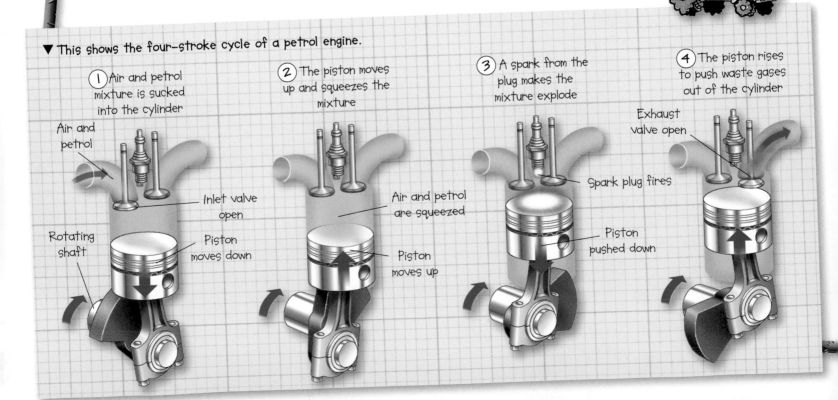

▼ This shows the four-stroke cycle of a petrol engine.

① Air and petrol mixture is sucked into the cylinder

② The piston moves up and squeezes the mixture

③ A spark from the plug makes the mixture explode

④ The piston rises to push waste gases out of the cylinder

Air and petrol

Inlet valve open

Rotating shaft

Piston moves down

Air and petrol are squeezed

Piston moves up

Spark plug fires

Piston pushed down

Exhaust valve open

▲ On a fast jet plane at full power, the exhaust gases from the engines glow almost white-hot.

16 A jet engine mixes air and kerosene and sets fire to it in one long, continuous, roaring explosion. Incredibly hot gases blast out of the back of the engine. These push the engine forward – along with the plane.

17 An electric motor passes electricity through coils of wire. This makes the coils magnetic, and they push or pull against magnets around them. The push-pull makes the coils spin on their shaft (axle).

▼ Using magnetic forces, an electric motor turns electrical energy into moving or kinetic energy.

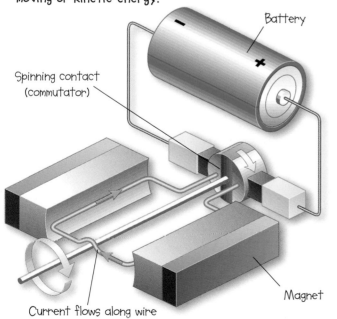

Battery

Spinning contact (commutator)

Current flows along wire

Magnet

18 Engines that burn fuel give out gases and particles through their exhausts. Some of these gases are harmful to the environment. The less we use engines, the better. Electric motors are quiet, efficient and reliable, but they still need fuel – to make the electricity at the power station.

▲ Electric cars have sets of batteries to turn the motor. The batteries are 'filled' with electrical energy by plugging into a recharging point.

QUIZ

1. Are exhaust gases good for the environment?

2. Does a diesel engine use sparks?

3. How many cylinders do most cars have?

4. Do electric cars have batteries?

Answers:
1. No, some of them are harmful
2. No 3. Four or six 4. Yes

Science on the move

19 Without science, you would have to walk everywhere, or ride a horse. Luckily, scientists and engineers have developed many methods of transport, most importantly, the car. Lots of people can travel together in a bus, train, plane or ship. These use less energy and resources, and make less pollution than cars.

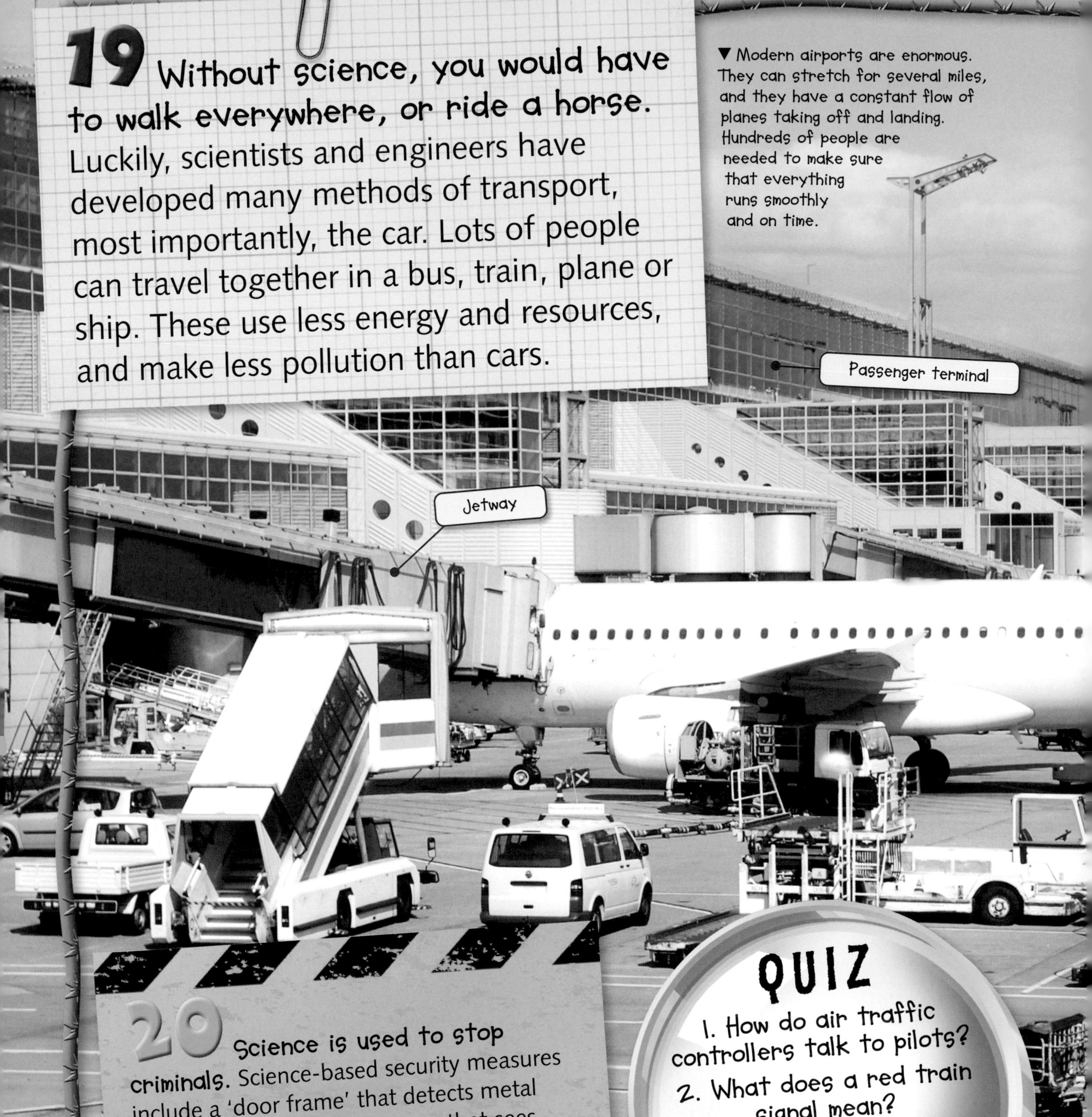

▼ Modern airports are enormous. They can stretch for several miles, and they have a constant flow of planes taking off and landing. Hundreds of people are needed to make sure that everything runs smoothly and on time.

Passenger terminal

Jetway

20 Science is used to stop criminals. Science-based security measures include a 'door frame' that detects metal objects like guns and a scanner that sees inside bags. A sniffer-machine can detect the smell of explosives or illegal drugs.

QUIZ
1. How do air traffic controllers talk to pilots?
2. What does a red train signal mean?
3. What powers the supports that move jetways?

Answers:
1. By radio 2. Stop 3. Electric motors

21 Jetways are extending walkways that stretch out from the passenger terminal right to the planes' doors. Their supports move along on wheeled trolleys driven by electric motors.

22 Every method of transport needs to be safe and on time. In the airport control tower, air traffic controllers track planes on radar screens. They talk to pilots by radio. Beacons send out radio signals, giving the direction and distance to the airport.

▶ The radar screen shows each aircraft as a blip, with its flight number or identity code.

IB-57
Q-74
CP-35
UA-154
L-47
AA-127
EJ-244
BA-76
BY-47
BA-277
RA-147
10 20 30 40 50 60
CP-87
Q-354
KL-163
AA-45
JAL-372
KL-89
L-178

23 On the road, drivers obey traffic lights. On a railway network, train drivers obey similar signal lights of different colours, such as red for stop. Sensors by the track record each train passing and send the information by wires or radio to the control room. Each train's position is shown as a flashing light on a wall map.

▼ Train signals show just two colours – red for stop and green for go.

D-27

▶ Trackside switches and detectors react to a train going past and automatically change the signals, so that a following train does not get too close.

02

24 Listening to the radio or television, playing music, shouting at each other – they all depend on the science of sound – acoustics. Sounds are carried by invisible waves in the air. The waves are areas of low pressure, where air particles are stretched farther apart, alternating with areas of high pressure, where they are squashed closer together.

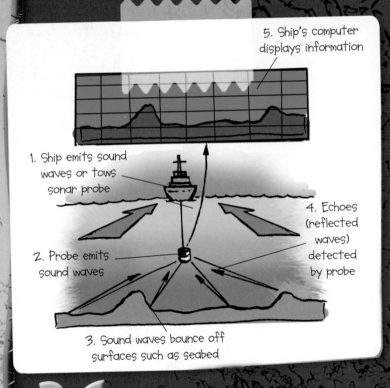

5. Ship's computer displays information

1. Ship emits sound waves or tows sonar probe

4. Echoes (reflected waves) detected by probe

2. Probe emits sound waves

3. Sound waves bounce off surfaces such as seabed

25 Scientists measure the loudness or intensity of sound in decibels, dB. A very quiet sound like a ticking watch is 10 dB. Ordinary speech is 50–60 dB. Loud music is 90 dB. A jet plane taking off is 120 dB. Too much noise damages the ears.

◀ In sonar (echo–sounding), sound waves in the water bounce or reflect off objects, and are detected.

Atomic explosion

26 Whether a sound is high or low is called its pitch, or frequency. It is measured in Hertz, Hz. A singing bird or whining motorcycle has a high pitch. A rumble of thunder or a massive truck has a low pitch. People can hear frequencies from 25 to 20,000 Hz.

Jet plane

Express train

Whisper

▶ The decibel scale measures the intensity, or energy, in sound.

| 0 dB | 40 dB | 80 dB | 120 dB | 180 dB |

27 Sound waves spread out from a vibrating object that is moving rapidly to and fro. Stretch an elastic band between your fingers and twang it. As it vibrates, it makes a sound. When you speak, vocal cords in your neck vibrate. You can feel them through your skin.

28 Sound waves travel about 330 metres every second. This is fast, but it is one million times slower than light waves. Sound waves also bounce off hard, flat surfaces. This is called reflection. The returning waves are heard as an echo.

29 Loudspeakers change electrical signals into sounds. The signals in the wire pass through a wire coil inside the speaker. This turns the coil into a magnet, which pushes and pulls against another magnet. The pushing and pulling make the cone vibrate, which sends sound waves into the air.

◄ The word 'sonic' means making sounds, and the high-pitched noises of bats can be described as 'ultrasonic' – too high for us to hear.

Echoes bouncing back off the moth

Sound waves from the bat

▲ Bats make high-pitched sounds. If the sounds hit an insect they bounce back to the bat's ears. The reflected sound (echo) gives the bat information about the size and location of the insect.

BOX GUITAR

You will need:
shoebox   elastic band
split pins   card

Cut a hole about 10 centimetres across on one side of an empty shoebox. Push split pins through either side of the hole, and stretch an elastic band between them. Pluck the band. Hear how the air and box vibrate. Cover the hole with card. Is the 'guitar' as loud?

Look out — light's about!

30 Almost everything you do depends on light and the science of light, which is called optics. Light is a form of energy that you can see. Light waves are made of electricity and magnetism – and they are tiny. About 2000 of them laid end to end would stretch across this full stop.

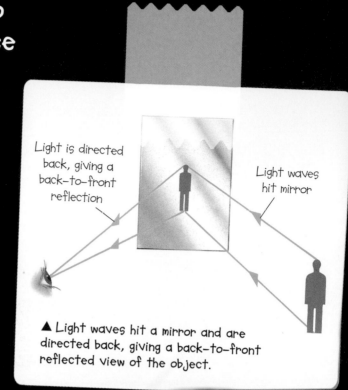

Light is directed back, giving a back-to-front reflection

Light waves hit mirror

▲ Light waves hit a mirror and are directed back, giving a back-to-front reflected view of the object.

▲ A prism of clear glass or clear plastic separates the colours in white light.

32 Like sound, light bounces off surfaces that are very smooth. This is called reflection. A mirror is smooth, hard and flat. When you look at it, you see your reflection.

31 Ordinary light from the Sun or from a light bulb is called white light. But when white light passes through a prism, a triangular block of clear glass, it splits into many colours. These colours are known as the spectrum. Each colour has a different length of wave. A rainbow is made by raindrops, which work like millions of tiny prisms to split up sunlight.

33 Light passes through certain materials, like clear glass and plastic. Materials that let light pass through, to give a clear view, are transparent. Those that do not allow light through, like wood and metal, are opaque.

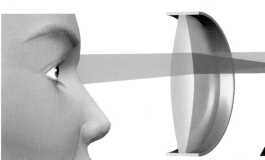

34 Mirrors and lenses are important parts of many optical (light-using) gadgets. They are found in cameras, binoculars, microscopes, telescopes and lasers. Without them, we would have no close-up photographs of tiny microchips or insects or giant planets – in fact, no photos at all.

I DON'T BELIEVE IT!
Light is the fastest thing in the Universe – it travels through space at 300,000 kilometres per second. That's seven times around the world in less than one second!

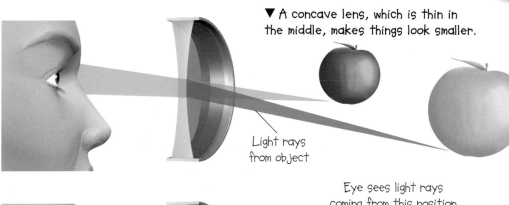

▼ A concave lens, which is thin in the middle, makes things look smaller.

Light rays from object

Eye sees light rays coming from this position

▲ A convex lens, which bulges in the middle, makes things look larger.

35 Light does not usually go straight through glass. It bends slightly where it goes into the glass, then bends back as it comes out. This is called refraction. A lens is a curved piece of glass or plastic that bends light to make things look bigger, smaller or clearer. Spectacle and contact lenses bend light to help people see more clearly.

▲ Glass and water bend, or refract, light waves. This makes a drinking straw look bent where it goes behind the glass and then into the water.

The power of lasers

36 Laser light is a special kind of light. Like ordinary light, it is made of waves, but it has three main differences. Ordinary white light is a mixture of colours, while laser light is one pure colour. Ordinary light waves have peaks (highs) and troughs (lows), which do not line up – laser light waves line up perfectly. Lastly, ordinary light spreads and fades. A laser beam can travel for thousands of kilometres as a strong, straight beam.

◀ The narrow horizontal beam from a laser spirit level can shine all the way across a building site.

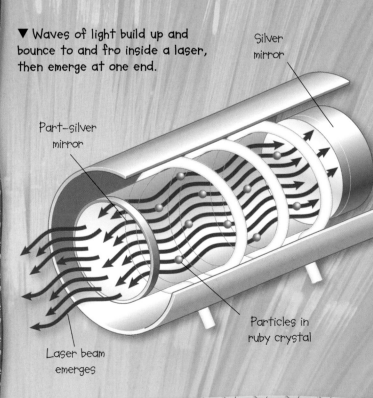

▼ Waves of light build up and bounce to and fro inside a laser, then emerge at one end.

Silver mirror

Part-silver mirror

Particles in ruby crystal

Laser beam emerges

37 To make a laser beam, energy is fed in short bursts into a substance called the active medium. The energy might be electricity, heat or ordinary light. In a red ruby laser, the active medium is a rod of ruby crystal. A strong lamp makes the particles in the crystal vibrate. The energy they give off bounces to and fro inside the crystal. Eventually, the rays vibrate with each other and they are all the same length. The energy becomes so strong that it bursts through a mirror at one end of the crystal.

Beam bounces off CD

Laser

Spinning CD

Reflected beam passes through prism

Laser beam bent by prism

Reflected beam detected by sensor

▲ A CD laser detects tiny pits in the disc's underside.

▲ In a spectacular outdoor light show, different coloured laser beams sweep to and fro as they pierce the darkness, seemingly all the way into space.

38 Lasers were invented in 1960. They are used to play CDs and DVDs for music and movies, and in computers. They cut through thick metal in factories, and carry out delicate eye operations. They carry phone calls and television programmes along cables. They even measure movements of the Earth to warn of volcanoes or earthquakes.

QUIZ

1. How far can laser beams travel?

2. When were lasers invented?

3. Which everyday machines use lasers?

Answers:
1. Thousands of kilometres 2. 1960 3. DVD players, CD players, computers

◀ An industrial laser has the power to melt metal into gas and cut a neat line.

Mysterious magnets

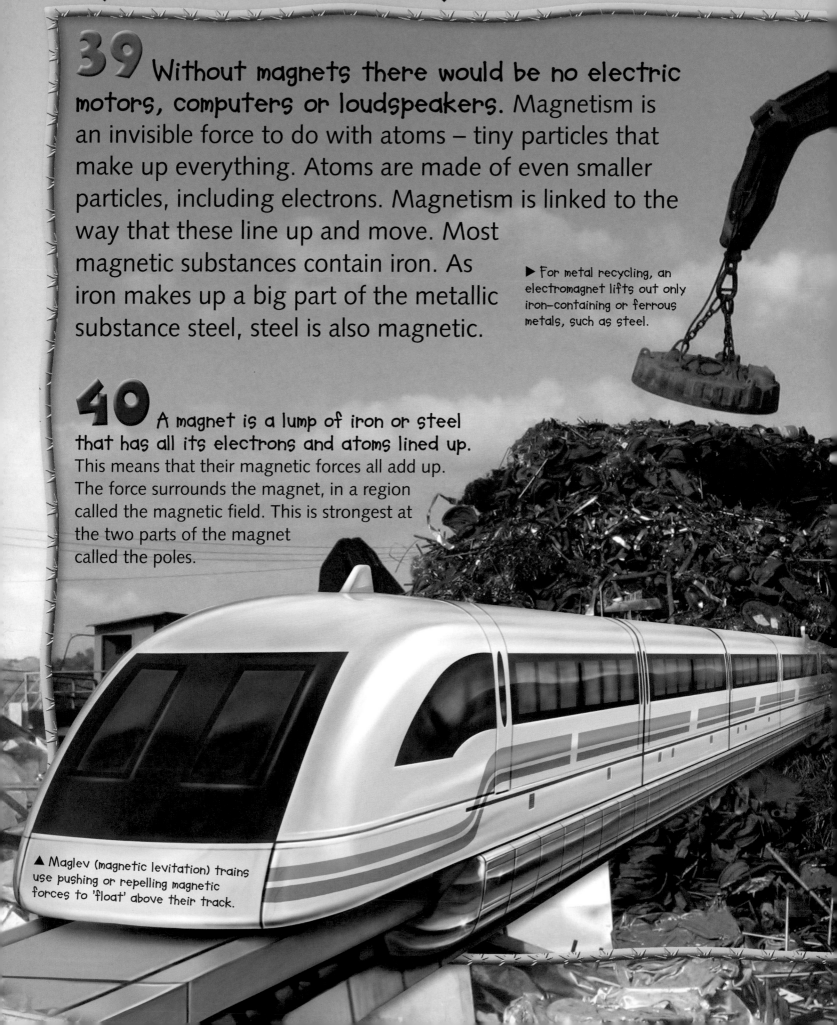

39 Without magnets there would be no electric motors, computers or loudspeakers. Magnetism is an invisible force to do with atoms – tiny particles that make up everything. Atoms are made of even smaller particles, including electrons. Magnetism is linked to the way that these line up and move. Most magnetic substances contain iron. As iron makes up a big part of the metallic substance steel, steel is also magnetic.

▶ For metal recycling, an electromagnet lifts out only iron-containing or ferrous metals, such as steel.

40 A magnet is a lump of iron or steel that has all its electrons and atoms lined up. This means that their magnetic forces all add up. The force surrounds the magnet, in a region called the magnetic field. This is strongest at the two parts of the magnet called the poles.

▲ Maglev (magnetic levitation) trains use pushing or repelling magnetic forces to 'float' above their track.

41 A magnet has two different poles – north and south. A north pole repels (pushes away) the north pole of another magnet. Two south poles also repel each other. But a north pole and a south pole attract (pull together). Both magnetic poles attract any substance containing iron, like a nail or a screw.

42 When electricity flows through a wire, it makes a weak magnetic field around it. If the wire is wrapped into a coil, the magnetism becomes stronger. This is called an electromagnet. Its magnetic force is the same as an ordinary magnet, but when the electricity goes off, the magnetism does too. Some electromagnets are so strong, they can lift whole cars.

▼ The field around a magnet affects objects that contain iron.

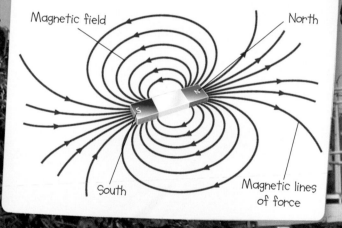

Magnetic field

North

South

Magnetic lines of force

QUIZ

Which of these substances or objects is magnetic?
1. Steel spoon 2. Plastic spoon
3. Pencil 4. Drinks can
5. Food can 6. Screwdriver
7. Cooking foil

Answers:
1. Yes 2. No 3. No 4. No 5. Yes 6. Yes 7. No

Electric sparks!

43 **Flick a switch and things happen.** The television goes off, the computer comes on, lights shine and music plays. Electricity is our favourite form of energy. We send it along wires and plug hundreds of machines into it.

▼ When an electric current flows, the electrons (small blue balls) all move the same way, jumping from one atom to the next. (The red balls are the centres or nuclei of the atoms.)

44 **Electricity depends on electrons.** In certain substances, when electrons are 'pushed', they hop from one atom to the next. When billions do this every second, electricity flows. The 'push' is from a battery or a generator. Electricity only flows in a complete loop or circuit. Break the circuit and the flow stops.

Atom

Electron

▼ Solar panels contain many hundreds of fingernail-sized PV (photovoltaic) cells. These convert light energy ('photo') to electrical energy ('voltaic').

▼ A battery has a chemical paste inside its metal casing.

Positive contact

Negative contact on base

45 **A battery makes electricity from chemicals.** Two different chemicals next to each other, such as an acid and a metal, swap electrons and get the flow going. Electricity's pushing strength is measured in volts. Most batteries are about 1.5, 3, 6 or 9 volts, with 12 volts in cars.

46 **Electricity flows easily through some substances, including water and metals.** These are electrical conductors. Other substances do not allow electricity to flow. They are insulators. Insulators include wood, plastic, glass, card and ceramics. Metal wires and cables have coverings of plastic, to stop the electricity leaking away.

47 Electricity from power stations is carried along cables on high pylons, or buried underground. This is known as the distribution grid. At thousands of volts, this electricity is extremely dangerous. For use in the home, it is changed to 220 volts (in the UK).

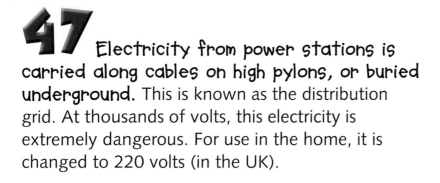

▼ Electricity generators are housed in huge casings, some bigger than trucks.

Pylun holds cables off the ground

◄ To check and repair high-voltage cables, the electricity must be turned off well in advance.

48 Mains electricity is made at a power station. A fuel such as coal or oil is burned to heat water into high-pressure steam. The steam pushes past the blades of a turbine and makes them spin. The turbines turn generators, which have wire coils near powerful magnets, and the spinning motion makes electricity flow in the coils.

MAKE A CIRCUIT

You will need:

lightbulb   battery   wire
plastic ruler   metal spoon   dry card

Join a bulb to a battery with pieces of wire, as shown. Electricity flows round the circuit and lights the bulb. Make a gap in the circuit and put various objects into it, to see if they allow electricity to flow again. Try a plastic ruler, a metal spoon and some dry card.

Making sounds and pictures

49 The air is full of waves we cannot see or hear, unless we have the right machine. Radio waves are a form of electrical and magnetic energy, just like heat and light waves, microwaves and X-rays. All of these are called electromagnetic waves and they travel at an equal speed – the speed of light.

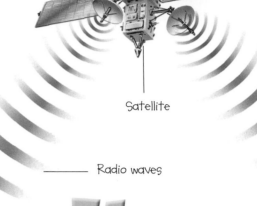

Satellite

Radio waves

51 Radio waves carry their information by being altered, or modulated, in a certain pattern. The height of a wave is called its amplitude. If this is altered, it is known as AM (amplitude modulation). Look for AM on the radio display.

50 Radio waves are used for both radio and television. They travel vast distances. Long waves curve around the Earth's surface. Short waves bounce between the Earth and the sky.

Aerial

52 The number of waves per second is called the frequency. If this is altered, it is known as FM (frequency modulation). FM radio is clearer than AM, and less affected by weather and thunderstorms.

▼ This range of waves, with different wavelengths, are electrical and magnetic energy. They are called the electromagnetic spectrum.

▲ A radio set picks up radio waves using its aerial or antenna.

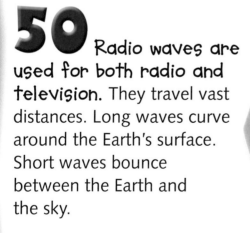

Long radio waves	Shorter radio waves (TV)	Microwaves	Infrared waves	Light waves (visible light)	Ultraviolet rays	X-rays	Short X-rays	Gamma rays

53 Radio waves are sent out, or transmitted, from antennae on tall masts or on satellites, to reach a very wide area. A radio receiver converts the pattern of waves to sounds. A television receiver or TV set changes them to pictures and sounds.

I DON'T BELIEVE IT!

You could send and receive radio signals on the Moon, but not in the sea. Radio waves travel easily through space, but only a few metres in water.

▼ A dish-shaped receiver picks up radio waves for TV channels.

54 Digital radio uses incredibly short bursts of radio waves with gaps between them – many thousands each second. Each burst represents the digit (number) 1, and a gap is 0. The order of the 1s and 0s carries information in the form of binary code, as in a computer.

▶ A plasma screen has thousands of tiny boxes, or cells, of three colours – red, green and blue. Electric pulses heat the gas inside for a split second into plasma, which gives out a burst of light. Combinations of these colours gives all the other colours.

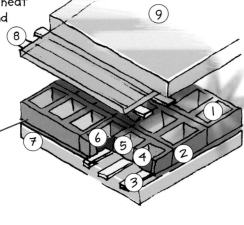

▼ Flat-screen TVs can be LCD or plasma. They use less electricity than cathode-ray TVs and produce a better picture.

KEY
① Glowing 'on' cell
② Dark 'off' cell
③ Rear grid of electrical contacts
④ – ⑥ Coloured phosphors inside cells
⑦ Backing plate
⑧ Front grid of electrical contacts
⑨ Transparent front cover

55 Computers are amazing machines, but they have to be told exactly what to do. So we put in instructions and information, by various means. These include typing on a keyboard, inserting a disc or memory stick, downloading from the Internet, using a joystick or games controller, or linking up a camera, scanner or another computer.

56 Most computers are controlled by instructions from a keyboard and a mouse. The mouse moves a pointer around on the screen and its click buttons select choices from lists called menus.

Flat screen monitor

USB (Universal Serial Bus) sockets

◄ This close up of a slice of silicon 'wafer' shows the tiny parts that receive and send information in a computer.

External monitor (screen) socket

Headphone socket

Silicon 'wafer'

Plastic casing

Wire 'feet' link to other part in the computer

57 Some computers are controlled by talking to them! They pick up the sounds using a microphone. This is speech recognition technology.

58 The 'main brain' of a computer is its Central Processing Unit. It is usually a microchip – millions of electronic parts on a chip of silicon, hardly larger than a fingernail. It receives information and instructions from other microchips, carries out the work, and sends back the results.

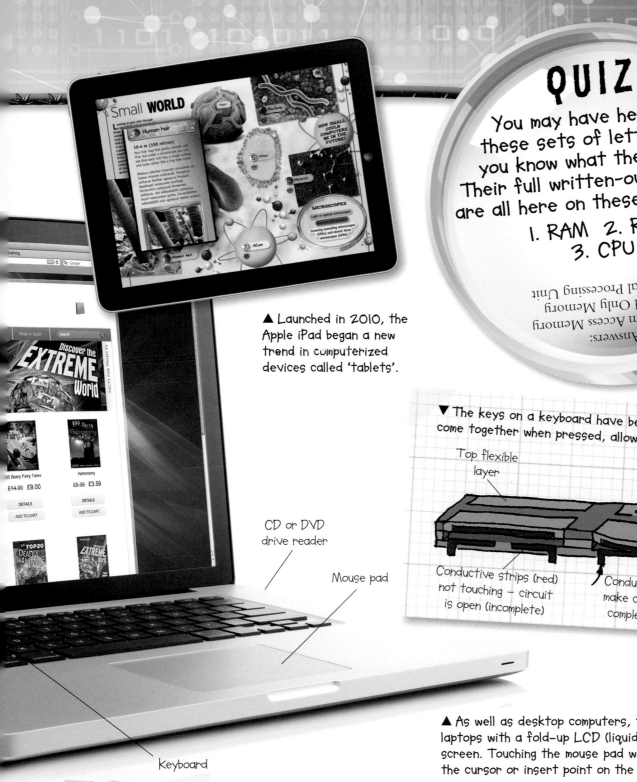

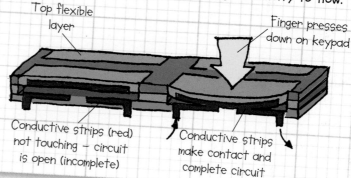

QUIZ

You may have heard of these sets of letters. Do you know what they mean? Their full written-out versions are all here on these two pages.

1. RAM 2. ROM
3. CPU

Answers:
1. Random Access Memory
2. Read Only Memory
3. Central Processing Unit

▲ Launched in 2010, the Apple iPad began a new trend in computerized devices called 'tablets'.

▼ The keys on a keyboard have bendy metal contacts that come together when pressed, allowing electricity to flow.

Top flexible layer

Finger presses down on keypad

Conductive strips (red) not touching – circuit is open (incomplete)

Conductive strips make contact and complete circuit

CD or DVD drive reader

Mouse pad

Keyboard

▲ As well as desktop computers, there are also laptops with a fold-up LCD (liquid crystal display) screen. Touching the mouse pad with a finger controls the cursor or insert point on the screen.

59 Information and instructions are contained in the computer in memory microchips.
There are two kinds. Random Access Memory is like a jotting pad. It keeps changing as the computer carries out its tasks. Read Only Memory is like an instruction book. It usually contains the instructions for how the computer starts up and how all the microchips work together.

60 A computer usually displays its progress on a monitor screen.
It feeds information to output devices such as printers, loudspeakers and robot arms. Information can be stored on CDs, DVDs, memory sticks (chips), external HDs (hard drive discs), or uploaded to the Internet.

Web around the world

61 The world is at your fingertips – if you are on the Internet. The Internet is one of the most amazing results of science. It is a worldwide network of computers, linked like one huge electrical spider's web.

62 Signals travel between computers in many ways. These include electricity along telephone wires, flashes of laser light along fibre-optic cables or radio waves between tall towers. Information is changed from one form to another in a split second. It can also travel between computers on different sides of the world in less than a second using satellite links.

First 'private' Internet, ARPANET, for the US military

Joint Academic Network (JANET) connects UK universities via their own Internet

Yahoo! Launches as a 'Guide to the World Wide Web' – what we now call a browser or search engine

Animation starts to become common on websites

1969   **1984**   **1994**   **1996**

1961   **1972**   **1989**   **1995**

First ideas for 'packet switching', the basic way the Internet parcels up and sends information in small blocks or packets

First emails, mostly on ARPANET

The birth of the Internet as we know it today, when Tim Berners-Lee and the team at CERN invent the World Wide Web to make information easier to publish and access

eBay and Amazon booksellers begin, and online trade starts to rise

63 The World Wide Web is public information that anyone can find on the Internet, available for everyone to see. However, sometimes you have to pay or join a club to get to certain parts of it. A website is a collection of related information, usually made up of text, videos and pictures. There might be hundreds of web pages within each website. Email is the system for sending private messages from one person to another.

I DON'T BELIEVE IT!

The World Wide Web is the best known and most widely used part of the Internet system. It has billions of pages of information.

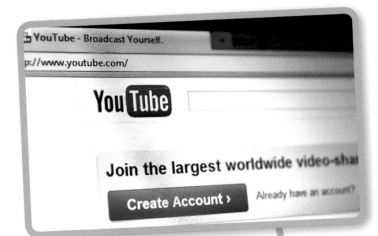

▼ Many mobile phones can be used to access the Internet, allowing users to browse web pages, send emails and watch videos.

Half of households in the UK have Internet connections

YouTube is launched, allowing video sharing

The first iPhones bring mobile Internet use for almost anyone

Facebook has fewer new users signing up – is the slower growth temporary, or the beginning of the end for online social networking?

2003 **2005** **2007** **2011**

1998 **2004** **2006** **2010**

Google is launched as a rival to Yahoo!

Facebook is launched, starting the trend for social networking over the Internet

Twitter is launched for posting and sharing text messages, but has a slow start

HD (High Definition) Internet video links become more practical

▲ The Web and the Internet interact with other technologies. Twitter is an online public version of text-only messages called 'tweets' developed from mobile phone 'texting' (SMS, Short Message Service).

64 You wouldn't make a bridge out of straw, or a cup out of bubblewrap! Choosing the right substance for the job is important. All the substances in the world can be divided into several groups. For example, metals such as iron, silver and gold are strong, hard and shiny, and conduct heat and electricity well. They are used to make things that have to be strong and long-lasting.

65 Plastics are made mainly from the substances in petroleum (crude oil). There are so many kinds – some are hard and brittle while others are soft and bendy. They are usually long-lasting, not affected by weather or damp, and they resist heat and electricity.

KEY

① The front wing is a special shape – this produces a force that presses the car down onto the track

② The main body of the car is made from carbon fibre, a light but very strong material

③ The car's axles are made from titanium – a very strong, light metal

④ The engine is made from various alloys, or mixtures of metals, based on aluminium. It produces up to ten times the power of a family car engine

⑤ Each tyre is made of thick, tough rubber to withstand high speeds

⑥ The rear wing is also carbon fibre composite

▼ A racing car has thousands of parts made from hundreds of materials. Each is suited to certain conditions such as stress, temperature and vibrations.

66 Ceramics are materials based on clay or other substances dug from the Earth. They can be shaped and dried, like a clay bowl. Or they can be fired – baked in a hot oven called a kiln. This makes them hard and long-lasting, but brittle and prone to cracks. Ceramics resist heat and electricity very well.

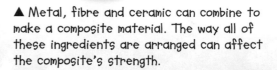

Metal

Fibre

Ceramic

▲ Metal, fibre and ceramic can combine to make a composite material. The way all of these ingredients are arranged can affect the composite's strength.

◀ In 2007, the Interstate 35W bridge collapsed in Minneapolis, USA, killing 13 people. It was due to cracking of small steel connecting plates that were too thin for the weight.

67 Glass is produced from the raw substances limestone and sand. When heated at a high temperature, these substances become a clear, gooey liquid, which sets hard as it cools. Its great advantage is that you can see through it.

68 Composites are mixtures or combinations of different materials. For example, glass strands are coated with plastic to make GRP – glass-reinforced plastic. This composite has the advantages of both materials.

MAKE YOUR OWN COMPOSITE

You will need:
flour   newspaper strips
water   balloon   pin

You can make a composite called pâpier maché from flour, newspaper and water. Tear newspaper into strips. Mix flour and water into a paste. Dip each strip in the paste and place it around a blown-up balloon. Cover the balloon and allow it to dry. Pop the balloon with a pin, and the composite should stay in shape.

World of chemicals

69 The world is made of chemical substances. Some are completely pure. Others are mixtures of substances – such as petroleum (crude oil). Petroleum provides us with thousands of different chemicals and materials, such as plastics, paints, soaps and fuels. It is one of the most useful, and valuable, substances in the world.

The fumes cool as they rise up the tower, causing them to condense

Petrol and vehicle fuels

Kerosene and medium fuels (jet fuel)

Heavy oils for lubrication

Furnace

Waxes, tars, bitumens, asphalts

▼ The biggest offshore oil platforms are more than 150 metres tall above the ocean surface. They drill boreholes into the seabed and pump up the crude oil, or petroleum.

Crude oil is super-heated and some parts turn into fumes

▲ The huge tower (fractionating column) of an oil refinery may be 100 metres high.

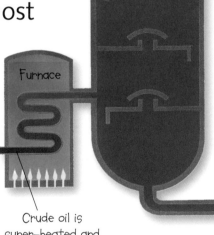

70 In an oil refinery, crude oil is heated in a huge tower. Some of its different substances turn into fumes and rise up the tower. The fumes condense (turn back into liquids) at different heights inside, due to the different temperatures at each level. Thick, gooey tars, asphalts and bitumens – used to make road surfaces – remain at the bottom.

71 One group of chemicals is called acids. They vary in strength from very weak citric acid, which gives the sharp taste to fruits such as lemons, to extremely strong and dangerous sulphuric acid in a car battery. Powerful acids burn and corrode, or eat away, substances. Some even corrode glass or steel.

72 Another group of chemicals is bases. They vary in strength from weak alkaloids, which give the bitter taste to coffee beans, to strong and dangerous bases in drain cleaners and industrial polishes. Bases feel soapy or slimy and, like acids, they can burn or corrode.

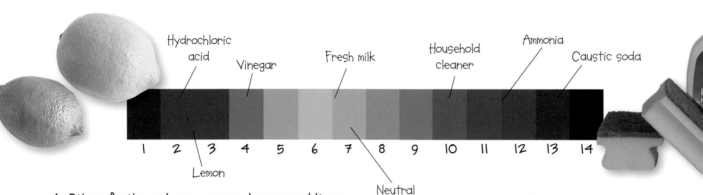

Hydrochloric acid   Vinegar   Fresh milk   Household cleaner   Ammonia   Caustic soda

1 2 3 4 5 6 7 8 9 10 11 12 13 14

Lemon

Neutral

▲ Citrus fruits such as oranges, lemons and limes have a tart taste because they contain a mild acid, called citric acid. It has a pH of 3.

▲ Household cleaners often contain alkalis to help them break down grease and fat. Some cleaners have a pH of 10.

Acidic substance

Neutral substance

Alkaline substance

► Indicator paper changes colour when it touches different substances. Acids turn it red, alkalis make it bluish–purple. The deeper the colour, the stronger the acid or base.

FROTHY FUN

You will need:
vinegar   washing soda

Create a chemical reaction by adding a few drops of vinegar to a spoonful of washing soda in a saucer. The vinegar is an acid, the soda is a base. The two react by frothing and giving off bubbles of carbon dioxide gas. What is left is a salt (but not to be eaten).

73 Acids and bases are 'opposite' types of chemicals. When they meet, they undergo changes called a chemical reaction. The result is usually a third type of chemical, called a salt. The common salt we use for cooking is one example. Its chemical name is sodium chloride.

74 The world seems to be made of millions of different substances – such as soil, wood, concrete, plastics and air. These are combinations of simpler substances. If you could take them apart, you would see that they are made of pure substances called elements.

1											
1 H Hydrogen											

	2										
3 Li Lithium	4 Be Beryllium										
11 Na Sodium	12 Mg Magnesium										

		3	4	5	6	7	8	9	10	11	12
19 K Potassium	20 Ca Calcium	21 Sc Scandium	22 Ti Titanium	23 V Vanadium	24 Cr Chromium	25 Mn Manganese	26 Fe Iron	27 Co Cobalt	28 Ni Nickel	29 Cu Copper	30 Zn Zinc
37 Rb Rubidium	38 Sr Strontium	39 Y Yttrium	40 Zr Zirconium	41 Nb Niobium	42 Mo Molybdenum	43 Tc Technetium	44 Ru Ruthenium	45 Rh Rhodium	46 Pd Palladium	47 Ag Silver	48 Cd Cadmium
55 Cs Caesium	56 Ba Barium	Elements 57–71	72 Hf Hafnium	73 Ta Tantalum	74 W Tungsten	75 Re Rhenium	76 Os Osmium	77 Ir Iridium	78 Pt Platinum	79 Au Gold	80 Hg Mercury
87 Fr Francium	88 Ra Radium	Elements 89–103	104 Rf Rutherfordium	105 Db Dubnium	106 Sg Seaborgium	107 Bh Bohrium	108 HS Hassium	109 Mt Meitnerium	110 Ds Darmstadtium	111 Rg Roentgenium	112 Cn Copernicum

Atomic number — Chemical symbol

20 Ca Calcium — Name

57 La Lanthanum	58 Ce Cerium	59 Pr Praseodymium	60 Nd Neodymium	61 Pm Promethium	62 Sm Samarium	63 Eu Europium	64 Gd Gadolinium	65 Tb Terbium
89 Ac Actinium	90 Th Thorium	91 Pa Protactinium	92 U Uranium	93 Np Neptunium	94 Pu Plutonium	95 Am Americium	96 Cm Curium	97 Bk Berkelium

▶ Stars are made mainly of burning hydrogen, which is why they are so hot and bright.

▲ The Periodic Table is a chart of all the elements. In each row the atoms get heavier from left to right. Each column (up–down) contains elements with similar chemical features. Every element has a chemical symbol, name, and atomic number, which is the number of particles called protons in its central part, or nucleus.

75 Hydrogen is the simplest element and it is the first in the Periodic Table. This means it has the smallest atoms. It is a very light gas, which floats upwards in air. Hydrogen was used to fill giant airships. But there was a problem – hydrogen catches fire easily and explodes.

76 About 90 elements are found naturally on and in the Earth. In an element, all of its particles, called atoms, are exactly the same as each other. Just as important, they are all different from the atoms of any other element.

Element types

- ■ Alkali metals
- □ Alkaline metals
- ■ Transition metals
- □ Other metals
- ■ Other non-metals
- ■ Halogens
- ■ Inert gases
- ■ Lanthanides
- ■ Actinides
- ■ Trans-actinides

Note: Elements 113–118 are synthetic elements that have only been created briefly, so their properties cannot be known for certain.

13	14	15	16	17	18
					2 He Helium
5 B Boron	6 C Carbon	7 N Nitrogen	8 O Oxygen	9 F Fluorine	10 Ne Neon
13 Al Aluminium	14 Si Silicon	15 P Phosphorus	16 S Sulphur	17 Cl Chlorine	18 Ar Argon
31 Ga Gallium	32 Ge Germanium	33 As Arsenic	34 Se Selenium	35 Br Bromine	36 Kr Krypton
49 In Indium	50 Sn Tin	51 Sb Antimony	52 Te Tellurium	53 I Iodine	54 Xe Xenon
81 Ti Thallium	82 Pb Lead	83 Bi Bismuth	84 Po Polonium	85 At Astatine	86 Rn Radon
113 Uut Ununtrium	114 Uuq Ununquadum	115 Uup Ununpentium	116 Uuh Ununhexium	117 Uus Ununsectium	118 Uuo Ununoctium

66 Dy Dysprosium	67 Ho Holmium	68 Er Erbium	69 As Arsenic	70 Yb Ytterbium	71 Lu Lutetium
98 Cf Californium	99 Es Einsteinium	100 Fm Fermium	101 Md Mendelevium	102 No Nobelium	103 Lr Lawrencium

QUIZ

1. How many elements are found naturally on Earth?
2. Which lightweight metal is very useful?
3. Which element makes up stars?
4. What do diamonds and coal have in common?

Answers:
1. About 90 2. Aluminium
3. Hydrogen 4. They are both made of pure carbon

78 Uranium is a heavy and dangerous element. It gives off harmful rays and tiny particles. This process is called radioactivity and it can cause sickness, burns and diseases such as cancer. Radioactivity is a form of energy and, under careful control, radioactive elements are used as fuel in nuclear power stations.

▶ Aluminium is a strong but light metal that is ideal for forming the body of vehicles such as planes.

77 Carbon is a very important element in living things – including our own bodies. It joins easily with atoms of other elements to make large groups of atoms called molecules. When it is pure, carbon can be two different forms. These are soft, powdery soot, and hard, glittering diamond. The form depends on how the carbon atoms join to each other.

79 Aluminium is an element that is a metal, and it is one of the most useful in modern life. It is light and strong, it does not rust, and it is resistant to corrosion. Saucepans, drinks cans, cooking foil and jet planes are made mainly of aluminium.

Bond (link)   Atom

◀ Diamond is a form of the element carbon where the atoms are linked, or bonded, in a very strong box-like pattern.

Small science

80 Many pages in this book mention atoms. They are the smallest bits of a substance. They are so tiny, even a billion atoms would be too small to see. But scientists have carried out experiments to find out what's inside an atom. The answer is – even smaller bits. These are sub-atomic particles, and there are three main kinds.

81 At the centre of each atom is a blob called the nucleus. It contains two kinds of sub-atomic particles. These are protons and neutrons. Protons are positive, or plus. The neutron is neither positive nor negative. Around the centre of each atom are sub–atomic particles called electrons. They whizz round the nucleus. In the same way that a proton in the nucleus is positive or plus, an electron is negative or minus. The number of protons and electrons is usually the same.

82 Atoms of the various elements have different numbers of protons and neutrons. An atom of hydrogen has just one proton. An atom of helium, the gas put in party balloons to make them float, has two protons and two neutrons. An atom of the heavy metal called lead has 82 protons and 124 neutrons.

I DON'T BELIEVE IT!

One hundred years ago, people thought the electrons were spread out in an atom, like the raisins in a raisin pudding.

Hydrogen   Helium   Oxygen

► The bits inside an atom give each substance its features, from exploding hydrogen to life–giving oxygen.

• Electron
• Proton
• Neutron

83 **It is hard to imagine the size of an atom.** A grain of sand, smaller than this o, contains at least 100 billion billion atoms. If you could make the atoms bigger, so that each one becomes as big as a pin head, the grain of sand would be 2 kilometres high!

Electron

Nucleus made from protons and neutrons

Movement of electrons

84 **'Nano' means one-billionth (1/1,000,000,000th), and nanotechnology is science at the smallest level – how atoms join to make molecules.** It is fairly new, but it has already produced many useful products, from stronger materials in jet planes and racing cars, to self-cleaning glass and bouncier tennis balls!

▲ The protons and neutrons in the nucleus of an atom are held together by a powerful force.

◀ This idea for a nano gear-bearing allows the central axle to spin inside the outer collar. It could be used in micromachines.

▼ Buckyballs are ball-shaped structures made of carbon atoms, used in some types of solar panels and medical research.

▶ Like buckyballs, nanotubes are formed mainly of carbon atoms. They can be combined with plastics in hi-tech equipment such as racing bicycles.

Scientists at work

85 There are thousands of different jobs and careers in science. Scientists work in laboratories, factories, offices, mines, steelworks, nature parks and almost everywhere else. They find new knowledge and make discoveries using a process called the scientific method.

86 First comes an idea, called a theory or hypothesis. This asks or predicts what will happen in a certain situation. Scientists continually come up with new ideas and theories to test. One very simple theory is – if I throw a ball up in the air, will it come back down?

▲ Some scientific work involves handling microbes or dangerous chemicals. This means safety precautions such as wearing gloves and a face mask may be necessary.

▶ In scientific terms, throwing a ball into the air is an experiment. What will be the result?

QUIZ
Put these activities in the correct order, so that a scientist can carry out the scientific method.
1. Results   2. Experiment
3. Conclusions   4. Theory
5. Measurements

Answer:
4, 2, 5, 1, 3

87 The scientist carries out an experiment or test, to check what happens. The experiment is carefully designed and controlled, so that it will reveal useful results. Any changes are carried out one at a time, so that the effect of each change can be studied. The experiment for our simple theory is – throw the ball up in the air.

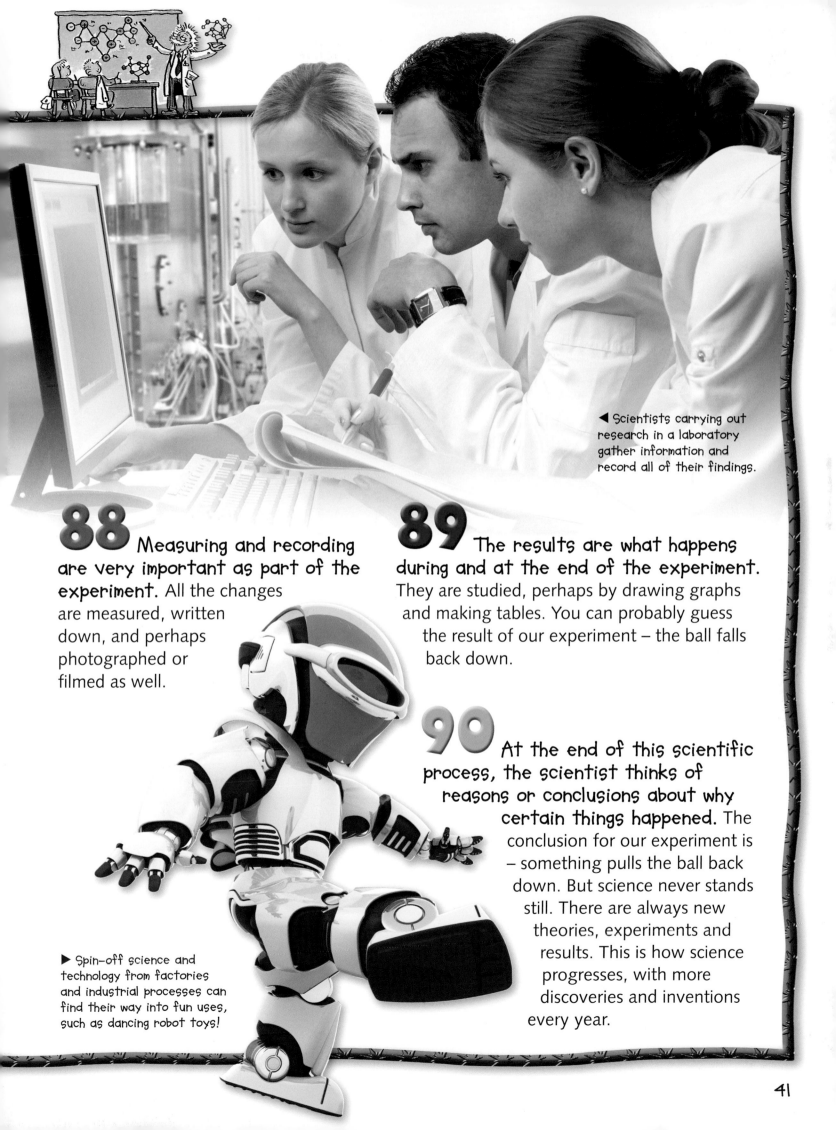

◄ Scientists carrying out research in a laboratory gather information and record all of their findings.

88 Measuring and recording are very important as part of the experiment. All the changes are measured, written down, and perhaps photographed or filmed as well.

89 The results are what happens during and at the end of the experiment. They are studied, perhaps by drawing graphs and making tables. You can probably guess the result of our experiment – the ball falls back down.

90 At the end of this scientific process, the scientist thinks of reasons or conclusions about why certain things happened. The conclusion for our experiment is – something pulls the ball back down. But science never stands still. There are always new theories, experiments and results. This is how science progresses, with more discoveries and inventions every year.

▶ Spin-off science and technology from factories and industrial processes can find their way into fun uses, such as dancing robot toys!

Science in nature

91 Science and its effects are found all over the natural world. Scientists study animals, plants, rocks and soil. They want to understand nature, and find out how science and its technology affect wildlife.

▼ One of the most important jobs in science is to study damage and pollution in the natural world. Almost everything we do affects wild places and animals and plants. For example, the power station here may make the river water warmer. This could encourage animals and plants accidentally introduced from tropical areas, which change the balance of nature.

92 One of the most complicated types of science is ecology. Ecologists try to understand how the natural world links together. They study how animals and plants live, what animals eat, and why plants grow better in some soils than others. They count the numbers of animals and plants and may trap animals briefly to study them, or follow the growth of trees in a wood. When the balance of nature is damaged, ecologists can help to find out why.

▼ The science of ecology involves long periods of studying nature in all kinds of habitats, from rivers to the seabed. For example, observing birds like herons, and fish such as trout, shows which foods they eat. This helps us to understand how changes to the habitat may affect them.

KEY
① Water beetle
② Rainbow trout
③ Water scorpion
④ Banded demoiselle damselfly
⑤ Heron
⑥ Otter
⑦ Warbler
⑧ Power station
⑨ Reedmace

I DON'T BELIEVE IT!

Science explains how animals such as birds or whales find their way across the world. Some detect the Earth's magnetism, and which way is north or south. Others follow changes in gravity, the force that pulls everything to the Earth's surface.

◀ Oil spills and leaks cause vast damage to a region's ecology. Scientists advise on the best ways to clear up the pollution.

93

Ecologists use many forms of high-tech science in their studies. They may fit an animal with a radio-collar so that its movements can be tracked. Special cameras see in the dark and show how night hunters catch their prey. Radar used to detect planes can also follow flocks of birds. The sonar (echo-sounding) equipment of boats can track shoals of fish or whales.

◀ Tracking tigers is vital to know the threats faced by these endangered big cats, and help to save them.

Body Science

94 One of the biggest areas of science is medicine. Medical scientists work to produce better drugs, more spare parts for the body and more machines for use by doctors. They also carry out scientific research to find out how people can stay healthy and prevent disease.

▲ Medical technology uses the latest equipment to diagnose illness, treat life-threatening conditions and cure diseases. This monitoring unit displays heart rate, pulse rate, amounts of oxygen in the blood, breathing speed, blood pressure and other vital signs.

95 As parts of the body work, such as the muscles and nerves, they produce tiny pulses of electricity. Pads on the skin pick up these pulses, which are displayed as a wavy line on a screen or paper strip. The ECG (electro-cardiograph) machine shows the heart beating. The EEG (electro-encephalograph) shows nerve signals flashing around the brain.

Laser beam hits retina inside eye

▶ A laser beam shines safely through the front of the eye to mend inner problems such as a detached retina.

96 Laser beams are ideal for delicate operations, or surgery, on body parts such as the eye. The beam makes very small, precise cuts. It can be shone into the eye and made most focused, or strongest, inside. So it can make a cut deep within the eye, without any harm to the outer parts.

▶ An endoscope is inserted into the body to give a doctor a picture on screen. The treatment can be given immediately.

MAKE A PULSE MACHINE

You will need:
modelling clay   drinking straw

Find your pulse by feeling your wrist, just below the base of your thumb, with a finger of the other hand. Place some modelling clay on this area, and stick a drinking straw into it. Watch the straw twitch with each heartbeat. Now you can see and feel your pulse. Check your pulse rate by counting the number of heartbeats in one minute.

97 The endoscope is like a flexible telescope made of fibre-strands. This is pushed into a body opening such as the mouth, or through a small cut, to see inside. The surgeon looks into the other end of the endoscope, or at a picture on a screen.

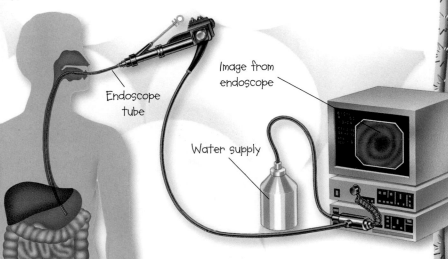

Image from endoscope

Endoscope tube

Water supply

Science in the Future

98 Many modern machines and processes can cause damage to our environment and our health. The damage includes acid rain, destruction of the ozone layer and the greenhouse effect, leading to climate change and global warming. Science can help to find solutions. New filters and chemicals called catalysts can reduce dangerous fumes from vehicle exhausts and power stations, and in the chemicals in factory waste pipes.

Fumes from power station cause acid rain

Oil storage tanks bring risk of leaks

◄ Fumes, waste and chemicals cause terrible pollution in many cities.

Intensive farming ruins soil

Ships may spill oil or fuel

QUIZ

If you become a scientist, which science would you like to study? See if you can guess what these sciences are:

1. Meteorology   2. Biology
3. Astronomy   4. Ecology

Answers:
1. Weather and climate
2. Animals, plants and other living things
3. Stars, planets and objects in space
4. The way nature works

Bottles crushed

Crushed glass
into furnace

Bottle bank for
empty glassware

Molten glass
poured into
moulds

Bottles cool
and glass
hardens

Bottles filled
and used

▶ Sorting waste
into different
materials such as
glass, plastic and
cardboard before it is
collected makes recycling
much more efficient.

▲ Recycling glass saves enormous
amounts of energy and raw materials.

99 One very important
area of science is recycling.
Many materials and substances can
be recycled – glass, paper, plastics,
cans, scrap metals and rags.
Scientists are working to improve
the process. Products should be
designed so that when they no
longer work, they are easy to
recycle. The recycling process itself
is also being made more effective.

100 We use vast amounts of
energy, especially to make electricity and
as fuel in our cars. Much of this energy comes
from crude oil (petroleum), natural gas and coal.
But these energy sources will not last for ever.
They also cause huge amounts of pollution.
Scientists are working to develop cleaner forms of
energy, which will produce less pollution and not
run out. These include wind power from turbines,
solar power from photocells, and hydroelectric
and tidal power from dams.

Rotor blade

Spinner

Pylon

▶ In a wind turbine, the
mechanical spinning movement
from the rotor is changed into
electrical energy.

Index

Page numbers in **bold** refer to main entries, those in *italics* refer to illustrations